# Some Words Tied Together Loosely

AJ Adams

Presentation by *BookLeaf Publishing*

Web: www.bookleafpub.com

E-mail: info@bookleafpub.com

ISBN: 9789357740227

First edition 2023

*This book is dedicated to everyone who has been kind to me.*

# The Devil Came Up

The devil came up from the ground
And all the mad dogs came roaming round
And you can still hear the sound
And you can still hear the sound

The devil came down from the sky
And the Earth she let out a cry
As a tear dripped from her eye
A tear dripped from her eye

The devil rose up from the river
And the bones fell with a shake and shiver
And you gave it up with a moan and a quiver
You gave it up with a moan and a quiver

The devil came home at last
All of his songs and stories now in the past
It all went by so fast
How did it all go by so fast

# A Big Mac Story

Went to get lunch at Mickey D's
Said no pickles, they forgot the cheese
Should've gone to Burger King

# Butterflying

Butterfly butterfly
With wings of yellow and green
Why do you pass me by
As you go your way unseen

So close to the earth
So close to the clouds
Your wings are your mirth
The skies are your shrouds

The flowers they see you dazing
They see you go by
Can you feel them gazing
Can you hear them cry

Butterfly, so beautiful and sublime
In ways you can't even know
Will you recall this in time
In time before you go?

# River Dances

She moves across the floor
Sliding on ice only she can see
The music crescendos, glissandos,
Mezzo pianos, mezzo fortes, mezzo mezzo
She knows them all
Even if you do not

But she's not really thinking about that
As the beat flashes green red blue
Green red blue and back again
Red, green and blue and back again,
And green, red, and blue again
No, she's not really thinking

She's dancing
She's dancing
Dance river dance
Dance river dance

# I Can't Be

5

I can't be your bunker
Your hideaway
Your cradle
Your safe space

I can't be your shelter
Your go-to
Your corner
Your knight in shining armor

I can't be your shoulder to cry on
Your protection
Your rock
Your escape from the world

I can't be something I'm not
I can't be
I can't be
I can't be yours

# Looking

Don't look at me like that
Searing eyes like a sidewalk in Miami in July
Looking glass on me got even Alice wondering

I can't see what you see
Don't know if I want to have to do you
Have you ever been told staring's not polite?

A mirror flesh-made man-made
Is what you must be looking for
To give your own reflection back in a new way

New ears, new nose, new cheekbones
Switch it all out or keep some leftovers,
It'll all be something different in the end

Or maybe that's not it at all
Maybe you don't even know where
Your pupils have stopped for a fraction of a
minute

But just for a second, just one second
I saw you, I saw me
Looking at what both of us wished we could se

# A Day

It's a lost day
The sun is almost gone
It's a lost day
Soon the moon will come

It's 5:00 here
The setting of the day
It's 5:00 somewhere
Down goes the sun and its rays

"Tomorrow will be different,"
Is what you proclaim
Tomorrow will be different
Or will it just be more of the same

# Pain is the Body

Pain is the body
The body is pain
Every step every inch
Feeling your life go down the drain

Like nails and a chalkboard
It forces itself together
In all kinds of situations
And all kinds of weather

You can try to outrun it
Outsmart it in some way
Avoid it or bribe it
Put it off for another day

But rich or poor, old or young
Black or white, short or tall
Quiet or loud, night or day
Pain comes for us all

# Sorry

9

Sorry I couldn't
reply to your text
I was thinking about
where I would sleep next

# I Can't

I can't keep up
With all the words on all the screens
All the faces in all the frames
I know they're just watching me

All the thoughts in my head
All the flashes in my pans
All the nerves in my system
I can't keep track

# The Hog

The hog doesn't fight
As he's being led away
The hog doesn't bite
On this, his final day

The hog doesn't cry
In the room with others
The hog lets time go by
With his sisters and brothers

The hog doesn't know
Who chose him or why
The hog can't go
Away, upwards into the sky

The hog recalls his time
In the mud, the grass
The hog knows this is fine
And soon all of this will pass

# The Passage/The Man

As he read from the passage
I felt the tears coming
To my eyes but they wouldn't
Leave so my face stayed dry

No one would know of my shame
My guilt my desire my envy
What was bubbling and boiling
Inside me all because I was reminded

Reminded of what I cannot be
Reminded of the man that isn't me

# Placeholder

This poem's a placeholder
A set of words to stand in line
To fill up some space
To fill up some time

This poem is meant to fill a gap
It's not anything much
It's not anything special
Just some words

# A Horse

14

A horse is a horse
Of course of course
Unless that horse
Of course of course
is a sea-horse

# She Sings To Me

15

I know she doesn't love me
Or anything like that
I know she doesn't want to
To call her mother

I know she doesn't sleep
I know she doesn't care
She doesn't even think of me

But to me, she speaks
To me, she gives herself away
To me, she goes on an on
To me, she sings

# How Do I Know

How do I know
How to do those things
Those things that
I don't know how to do

Just knowing is not
The solution or the answer
It can't be
But I wish it was

# More Time

There's always more time
More time to do the things
you said you were going to
There's always more time

There are always more things
More things to do
More things to be done
There are always more things

More lessons to learn
More people to meet
More bills to pay
More money to make

There's always more time
To do more of the things
That you want to do
There's always more time,
Until there isn't

# Something Triumphant

I wanted to write something
at the end here
Something triumphant
Something profound

Something with a real pow!
Something to make you
the reader, go,
"Wow!"

But I don't have anything like that
So you can just go ahead and
Close this book

Or just skip to the last page
If you're reading the e-book version